S0-FQZ-825

Thank you for purchasing this practice exam. Hopefully you'll find it to contribute to your success in passing the CIPT exam. The questions of this practice exam have been phrased to come as close as possible to the type, ambiguity and difficulty of the questions you will face on the CIPT exam, including a number of scenario questions.

The content of this practice exam is based on the latest exam blueprint to make sure that all domains are covered. In addition, the questions of the different domains have been mixed to disrupt the flow and train your brain to switch between domains.

There are no instructions on how to take this practice exam, because whether you use pen and paper or write in this document (hopefully not on your e-reader) is completely up to you. However, flagging questions can be extremely useful. Train yourself in marking a question you don't immediately know the answer to in order to get back to it later (if you have time left), and you will greatly increase your chances of passing the exam.

There are 90 questions, for which you can take 2,5 hours. The available information regarding the percentage of questions you'll need to answer correctly is vague, but if you score about 80% you should be ready.

The first part of this document contains the practice exam, followed by the answer key. The second part contains the same questions, with the correct answer marked and some more information to lead you to the correct answer, as well as to show you how you could have been tricked into choosing the incorrect answer.

Good luck!

1. What is most likely the reason for not paying hackers after a ransomware attack?
A. A complete backup is available at an offline location
B. There is not enough money available
C. The request by the hackers is for a certain amount of Bitcoin
D. Paying the hackers after a ransomware attack is likely illegal

2. Which of the following most likely failed when an employee's password is guessed by a hacker based on information obtained about him/her?
A. Access controls
B. Social engineering prevention
C. Software protection
D. Auditing

3. What is the Payment Card Industry Data Security Standard?
A. A US law
B. An EU law
C. A comprehensive law
D. Self-regulation

4. Which of the following is a privacy advantage of masking (part of) an IP address?
A. Masking provides protection against cyber attacks
B. Masking secures the connection by anonymization
C. The IP address is less likely to constitute personal data
D. Masking speeds up the connection due to a reduction in information that is transferred

5. What is the least likely reason to use easy to understand language in a privacy notice?
A. The General Data Protection Regulation requires clear and plain language
B. Users are less likely to read it
C. Users are more likely to grasp the full extent of the data processing
D. Several US laws require clear and conspicuous privacy policies/notices

6. What would be the best moment to show the privacy notice for a consumer software program?
A. During setup
B. Before setup
C. Before purchase
D. Before first use

7. Which of the following is likely not a risk an IT manager has to deal with?
A. Improper access to data
B. Privacy by Design
C. Data breaches
D. Incorrect retention periods

Use this case for the following three questions:

Amidst the craze for mobile phone application development, you and a few friends had the brilliant idea to develop an application that allows users to find single people in the area. You develop the application and witness the user base expanding rapidly and the application becoming the most popular dating application worldwide.

You struggle to keep the application online though, as mobile advertisement delivery is cumbersome, and is detrimental to user experience. Due to this, one of the other developers comes with the brilliant idea to analyze the data of users and create a database full of qualities that people in specific areas have.

After setting up meetings with potential buyers for the analysis data, it appears to be a great source of income. The application is stripped of its advertisements for an optimal user experience, and the new update enables the collection of more types of data about the user.

8. Where would the specifics of what is being done be mentioned for the users in the European Union?
A. In the privacy notice, to be made available before starting to collect data
B. As no consent is required, there is no need to inform the users of the data collection
C. Only the data collection that cannot reasonably be expected needs to be communicated to the user, which may be unnecessary in this case
D. Only for the paid version of the application is such communication required

9. If the application makes decision automatically, such as which users to connect to which other user, what can be said about that practice?
A. This is a form of processing that does not need to be communicated
B. This likely constitutes automated decision-making
C. If this is a technology-enabled process, it is not processing of personal data since no person is involved
D. A contract with the user is required to continue this practice

10. When designing the dating application, which of the following would be the best example of Privacy by Design?
A. Allowing a user to stop the application accessing the user's photos
B. Allowing a user to stop the application accessing the user's contacts
C. No unnecessary connections between the application and the user's device
D. Using a third party for the payment process for the customers that elect to use the paid version of the application

11. What is cyphertext best described as?
A. Random data on a hard drive
B. A list of passwords
C. An encryption tool
D. Unreadable seemingly random data

12. Receiving a text message with a passcode after entering your password is which of the following?
A. Two-way protection
B. Two-way authentication
C. Encrypted transmission
D. Multi-factor authentication

13. Which of the following best describes encryption?
A. Compressed data
B. Data requiring a key
C. Randomized data
D. Empty file storage

14. Which of the following does not refer to access control within an organization?
A. Role-based access control
B. Person-based access control
C. CEO overruling for processing of personal data
D. Restricting certain levels of the organization from file access

15. Which of the following is least likely a risk of the Internet of Things?
A. Persons not being able to request access to their personal data
B. Accidentally collecting data that is not allowed to be collected
C. Being able to link data to uncover more information inadvertently
D. An inadequate level of risk being assigned to the collected data

16. Which of the following is least likely effective in preventing access to data by an intruder?
A. Poor access controls
B. A virus
C. A password policy
D. A stolen computer

17. What is the most likely risk of over securing data?
A. Attracting hackers to the data
B. Overloading the firewall
C. Ignored access control policies
D. Productivity is reduced

18. What is the security advantage of using cables instead of wireless internet?
A. Data transfers can take place at a higher speed
B. An intruder would more likely need physical access in order to intercept data
C. No firewall is required
D. Password policies can be simplified

19. When would an organization most likely use a bastion server?
A. When there are a large number of applications that cannot run only on individual computers
B. When you wish to enhance security by scanning all incoming data
C. When it is too expensive to install solid-state drives in al computers
D. When access controls need to be applied uniformly for all programs

20. What is the best way to determine whether a privacy policy applies to a file on the network of an organization?
A. An analysis performed by the Chief Information Security Officer
B. A digital Data Protection Officer signature
C. A server scan on the size and date of the data
D. Classifying the data

21. How is it most likely called when no names are present in a dataset but linking it with another dataset results in identification of the data subjects in the dataset?
A. Anonymization
B. Pseudonymization
C. Encryption
D. Compression

22. When a video of someone is posted and that person was not the original subject of the video but their face was placed on the original subject, what is this most likely called?
A. A deep fake
B. A facetime video
C. Corrupted data
D. A data breach

23. Which of the following is an example of a nudge?
A. A login requirement to access your social media account
B. A reminder of the consequences before allowing or starting a process
C. An IP verification before a social media post gets processed
D. A multi-factor authentication requirement before accessing your social media account

24. Which of the following is not a common privacy dark pattern?
A. Anchoring
B. Distractions and delays
C. Framing
D. Cumbersome privacy choices

25. If you are asked, when reacting to an online advertisement, to transfer 1 cent to confirm your identity, but you are sent a fake link so as to lure you into exposing your password, what is that called?
A. Spear phishing
B. Phishing
C. Spam
D. Malware

26. Which of the following is most important for anti-malware software?
A. A dedicated server
B. Access to browser history
C. Access to personal data
D. Up-to-date signatures

27. In which of the following cases does the IP address of a VPN most likely constitute, or lead to collecting, personal data?
A. When using a VPN to spoof the region so you can access content of a that region
B. When having paid for the access to the VPN with a personal credit card
C. When someone uses a VPN to access their e-mail inbox
D. When only one person uses the VPN

28. What are maximum tries and account lockout?
A. Password heuristics
B. Standard practice
C. Malware protection
D. Authentication rules

29. What is the most effective way of preventing private data from leaving an organization's server?
A. Using a malware scanner
B. Using a virus scanner
C. Network-level data loss prevention technologies using a scanner
D. Role-based access control

30. Which of the following describes a zero-day threat?
A. A known weakness in a software package
B. A postponed software update
C. An unsecure http connection as part of a startup protocol
D. An unknown weakness in software

31. What gets transmitted over a network with VoIP?
A. Voice communication
B. IP addresses
C. Viruses
D. Virus signatures

32. How can you protect files after they are copied to a different device?
A. Digital Rights Management
B. Secure transfer
C. Anonymization
D. De-identification

33. Which of the following is the least likely reason organizations use cloud storage?
A. Enhanced security
B. Better access to data
C. Lower costs of data storage
D. Improvements in data recovery

34. Which of the following will privacy policies least likely aid in?
A. Financial risk reduction
B. Security risk reduction
C. Legal risk reduction
D. Brand risk reduction

35. What can be an issue with organizational privacy training?
A. Privacy practices of other teams are not always covered
B. E-learning is not effective
C. Even after a privacy incident, CEOs are reluctant to approve privacy training
D. If a security training is already in place, there can be a lot of overlap

36. Which of the following does not prevent raw data from being accessed?
A. Homomorphic encryption
B. Multiparty computation
C. Differential privacy
D. Compression

37. Which of the following permits defining group policies?
A. HTTPS
B. HTTP
C. Microsoft SQL
D. Virtual Private Network

38. What is COBIT5?
A. A standard for privacy policies
B. A standard for privacy notices
C. A guide for 256-bit encryption
D. A framework of security controls

39. Which of the following will you least likely find in an organization's privacy notice?
A. The type of data collected
B. How to make use of your rights
C. Where a complaint can be made
D. The privacy officer of the processor

40. When a website allows you to click on the topics you want information on, what is this likely called?
A. A privacy policy
B. A layered privacy notice
C. A cookie wall
D. Privacy Icons

41. What can a privacy policy do for an organization that develops one?
A. Identify privacy gaps within an organization
B. Ensure compliance with relevant legislation
C. Set the tone across the organization
D. Prevent data breaches and fines

42. What is an agreement with a third-party processing data on an organization's behalf called?
A. Binding Corporate Rules
B. A binding privacy agreement
C. A data processing agreement
D. A contractor agreement

43. Under the General Data Protection Regulation, how many days does an organization have, to respond to a data access request?
A. Twenty-five days
B. Twenty working days
C. A month
D. Two months

44. What can the act of labelling a file high, moderate of low be considered?
A. Data classification
B. Processing of personal data
C. Processing of personal information
D. Data collection

Use this case for the following three question:

A new video streaming service is providing customers with free trials for a limited time. They do this in the testing phase, and also specify to the customers that the streaming service is still in the testing phase.

During the testing phase, a large amount of new content is delivered to the first users in the form of TV shows and movies. The streaming service uses all kinds of data from the users to analyze the performance of its service, as well as the quality of its content.

One of the ways the streaming service uses users for determining the quality of its content, is by accessing the camera in the smart TV, laptop or mobile device of the user. The application of the streaming service contains emotion-recognition software, which analyses the facial expressions of the users. This is then sent as feedback, as a replacement of organizing a focus group.

45. What kind of data is the facial recognition software processing?
A. Biometric data
B. Physical data
C. Legal data
D. Digital imagery

46. A group of hackers accessed the servers of the streaming service and has stolen a large amount of user data. Which of the following is likely true?
A. Since the streaming service was free, no guarantees can be provided for the user's privacy, and there are no legal obligations resting on the streaming service
B. If the hackers are paid to delete the data, no further action is required
C. The streaming service has to organize a press conference to inform the public
D. The streaming service will have to report this to a Data Protection Authority

47. For the storage of the results of the analysis as regards viewing history, which of the following is likely required in the European Union?
A. Consent is required
B. A data processing agreement is required
C. No processors may be used
D. Storage is not processing, so only storing the data without further use requires no action

48. When only certain types of employees have access to certain data, what is this called?
A. Multi-factor authentication
B. Role-based access control
C. Three prong authentication
D. Person-based access control

49. What is the period of an organization's data retention least likely influenced by?
A. Processing requirements
B. Organization resources
C. Regulatory requirements
D. Data classification

50. How can data aggregation best be described?
A. The scrambling of data to make it unreadable without a key
B. The removal of names
C. The removal of all identifiers in a dataset
D. A reflection of attributes with a certain level of granularity

51. Which of the following is least likely a risk when deleting data in an organization?
A. That an update in the data inventory is required due to the deleted data
B. That the data is present at other points in the organization
C. That there is still a legal requirement to keep the data
D. That a copy exists in a backup

52. Which of the following is the least likely risk if an organization loses data stored on a thumb drive?
A. A data breach for data with lower levels of encryption
B. Permanent loss of data due to not having a backup
C. Being left with outdated data
D. Losing track and not obliging with a request for deletion

53. How can a browser be identified based on its unique settings?
A. VPN spoofing
B. Browser fingerprinting
C. A malware infection
D. Through an Internet Explored Exploit

54. When only users from a certain location can access a file, what is this called?
A. Geo-favoring
B. Virtual Private Network
C. Two-factor authentication
D. Attribute-based access control

55. What are Secure Sockets Layer and Transport Layer Security?
A. These are website tools
B. These are persistent cookies
C. These are functional cookies
D. These are types of protocols

56. Which of the following results in data that cannot be decrypted?
A. Asymmetric encryption
B. Symmetric encryption
C. Hashing
D. Compression

57. When you are at work and login once, providing you with access to e-mail, work-time registration, etcetera, what is this generally referred to?
A. Multi-factor authentication
B. Multi-platform authentication
C. Single-sign on
D. Multi-user authentication

58. What is a brute force attack, with current (2020) level technology, most useful for?
A. Cracking simple passwords
B. Matching asymmetric encryption keys
C. Deciphering encryption
D. Generating cheat codes for new gaming consoles

59. Which of the following statements is least true about incident response in a typical organization?
A. The Data Protection Officer runs the show after an incident
B. It is a joint effort to guide the organization in the correct response
C. Privacy is not necessarily the most important part of the incident response strategy
D. It is the head of the organization that ultimately decides which course to take

60. Which of the following is most important for the systems development lifecycle from a General Data Protection Regulation perspective?
A. Approval of the Data Protection Officer
B. Involvement of the Data Protection Officer
C. Privacy by Design
D. A Privacy Impact Assessment

61. Which of the following is not a way for an organization to address privacy risk?
A. Transfer
B. Assess
C. Accept
D. Mitigate

62. Which of the following is true about the Personal Information Protection and Electronic Documents Act?
A. Organizations must obtain at least opt-out consent before processing
B. The Personal Information Protection and Electronic Documents Act applies only to government agencies
C. The Personal Information Protection and Electronic Documents Act is a South African law
D. The Personal Information Protection and Electronic Documents Act is a Singaporean law

63. Which of the following is not part of the information lifecycle?
A. Retention
B. Destruction
C. Consent
D. Use

64. IT security measures in an organization likely have the most impact on which of the following?
A. Use limitation
B. Data quality
C. Accountability
D. Security safeguards

65. Which of the following types of cookies most likely does not require consent?
A. Functional cookies
B. Analytical cookies
C. Marketing cookies
D. Tracking cookies

66. What is the most likely reason for choosing a reputable third party to procure data from?
A. Data security
B. Collection limitation
C. The correct legal basis
D. Data quality

67. When requesting a third party, in the European Union, to collect information about local individuals for your organization which of the following is not necessarily important?
A. A Data Protection Officer
B. Adequate security
C. A privacy Notice
D. A data processing agreement

68. Which of the following is true for personal data that has fulfilled the purpose it was collected for?
A. It can be kept only if consent is provided
B. System limitations provide a valid reason to postpone deletion
C. It can be stored up to 10 years
D. There is likely no legal basis for further processing in its current form

69. Which of the following is least likely deduced from a person's web browsing history?
A. Employment status
B. Sexual preference
C. Medical condition
D. Exact financial data

70. Which of the following can be said about hard copies containing personal data?
A. They are unregulated as they are not digital
B. No security is possible as there cannot be an audit trail
C. They can be part of a data breach
D. They fall outside the scope of the General Data Protection Regulation

71. What is likely the best way to test software that processes personal data?
A. Use data without names
B. Acquire consent for testing
C. Encrypt the data before testing
D. Use dummy data

72. When composing a transfer agreement, from a privacy perspective, which of the following is the most important element?
A. The processing fee
B. The file types used
C. The processing limitations
D. The encryption method

73. Which of the following best describes a data retention period?
A. The maximum period of time data should be kept
B. A set time to destruct the data
C. A set time before encryption
D. Storage space

74. Which of the following is most true about business continuity and disaster recovery strategies?
A. They require Data Protection Officer approval
B. Most privacy laws require at least one of the two
C. They must be continually reviewed
D. Most privacy laws require both

75. Which of the following is least likely going to cause a new issue when starting to use data centers instead of one local server?
A. The encryption method used to protect the data
B. The legislation that has become applicable
C. Physical security of the data centers
D. Data processing agreements, if outsourced

76. When can data about the functioning of a vendor be considered personal data under the General Data Protection Regulation?
A. When there is only one employee working for that company
B. When no data processing agreement is in place
C. When a lower standard of encryption is used
D. The moment consent is obtained

Use this case for the following three question:

A virus breaks out in Asia. The virus is dangerous to the elderly but spreads through people of all ages. Slowly, the virus is spreading from Asia to the rest of the world and starts claiming lives.

As a result of the virus people are frantic and overly cautious. This has led to people calling in sick, not going to school or work. Public spaces are becoming deserted as well, and the economy is slowly crumbling, small business owners being the first to collapse.

To combat the loss in productivity, many of the larger organizations are asking their employees to work from home. They provide teleworking equipment, either to be installed on their own personal computer or on a computer the organization provides.

77. In order to establish a secure connection, a program is provided that connects to the organization's network and through that connects to the internet, making it appear as if the IP address used by the employees is the IP address of the organization. What can this be called?
A. Multi-factor authentication
B. Network spoofing
C. IP address masking
D. The use of a VPN

78. An external server hosts all working documents that employees need to do their job, which all can access at the same time from a distance. What can the storage on an external server be called?
A. Encryption
B. Intranet
C. File access audit trail
D. Cloud computing

79. When using a company provided computer, the webcam in the laptop is accessible to the company's IT personnel. Where would this information most likely be found?
A. In the employment contract
B. In a privacy notice provided with the company computer
C. In labor law
D. In the organization's privacy policy

80. Which is not a commonly used form of authentication?
A. Something you know
B. Something you have
C. Where you are
D. Metadata

81. Which of the following is not a single sign-on technology?
A. OpenID Federation
B. Liberty Alliance
C. Identity Metasystem Architecture
D. Microsoft Access

82. Which of the following is an example of Software as a Service?
A. Windows 10
B. Software on a USB drive
C. Office 365
D. Software downloaded from the cloud to install

83. What is an example of a demilitarized zone network?
A. Public WIFI
B. A third amendment server
C. A pay network
D. A store's separate network for customers only

84. Which of the following is a pass phrase?
A. @lRightyTh3n
B. 124590MAX
C. Milkwaukee
D. HappyDayCongruencyHorse

85. A fingerprint is an example of which of the following?
A. Biometrics
B. Multi-factor authentication
C. Password replacement
D. Location data

86. Which of the following is an example of the privacy paradox?
A. Staying away from all social media because you do not want your data shared
B. Opting out of location tracking on social media, but publicly checking-in to every hotel and restaurant you visit
C. Not allowing a social media application to access your photos, but having over a terabyte of photos on your mobile device
D. Refusing to share your sexual preference on a social media website, but then joining another social media website specific for a certain sexual preference

87. What gets inserted during an SQL injection?
A. Commands
B. A form
C. Malware
D. Executable files

88. What can most likely be said about web beacons?
A. Web beacons cannot track you
B. Web beacons are exactly the same as a cookie
C. A web beacon is malware
D. Web beacons are not visible to the naked eye

89. If your web browser allows for the option to send a signal not to place tracking cookies, what would this be called?
A. Privacy by Design
B. Opt-in
C. Opt-out
D. Do Not Track

90. How can cloud computing best be described?
A. Third party involved processing
B. Local Area Network
C. Using servers on the internet to do your work
D. Storage expansion

Answers:
1A, 2B, 3D, 4C, 5B, 6C, 7B, 8A, 9B, 10C, 11D, 12D, 13B, 14C, 15A, 16C, 17D, 18B, 19A, 20D, 21B, 22A, 23B, 24A, 25B, 26D, 27D, 28D, 29C, 30D, 31A, 32A, 33A, 34B, 35A, 36D, 37C, 38D, 39D, 40B, 41C, 42C, 43C, 44A, 45A, 46D, 47A, 48B, 49B, 50D, 51A, 52B, 53B, 54D, 55D, 56C, 57C, 58A, 59A, 60C, 61B, 62A, 63C, 64D, 65A, 66D, 67A, 68D, 69D, 70C, 71D, 72C, 73A, 74C, 75A, 76A, 77D, 78D, 79B, 80D, 81D, 82C, 83D, 84D, 85A, 86B, 87A, 88D, 89D, 90C

Explanations:

1. What is most likely the reason for not paying hackers after a ransomware attack?

A. A complete backup is available at an offline location (correct)
B. There is not enough money available
C. The request by the hackers is for a certain amount of Bitcoin
D. Paying the hackers after a ransomware attack is likely illegal

More information:
Of the options provided, A is the most likely reason. During a ransomware attack, files are encrypted by hackers and an organization is asked for money in order to decrypt the files. This means you will lose access to your files if you do not have another copy. So, having a backup is the best solution. An offline backup is the best, as this cannot be accessed by hackers from a distance, hence the risk of losing these files is lower.

2. Which of the following most likely failed when an employee's password is guessed by a hacker based on information obtained about him/her?

A. Access controls
B. Social engineering prevention (correct)
C. Software protection
D. Auditing

More information:
When a password is guessed by a hacker based on information about him/her, the hacker likely figured this information out through social engineering. This can be through contacting the person and gathering information about him/her, or contacting others and gathering information about the target. Option B is the correct answer.

3. What is the Payment Card Industry Data Security Standard?
A. A US law
B. An EU law
C. A comprehensive law
D. Self-regulation (correct)
More information:
The Payment Card Industry Data Security Standard is not a law, and it is developed by the payment card industry itself. It is thus the industry regulating itself, which is referred to as self-regulation. Option D is the correct answer.

4. Which of the following is a privacy advantage of masking (part of) an IP address?
A. Masking provides protection against cyber attacks
B. Masking secures the connection by anonymization
C. The IP address is less likely to constitute personal data (correct)
D. Masking speeds up the connection due to a reduction in information that is transferred
More information:
When (part of) an IP address is masked, part of the address is removed/replaced. This makes the IP address less unique and therefore less likely to be tied to only one person. Option C is the correct answer.

5. What is the least likely reason to use easy to understand language in a privacy notice?
A. The General Data Protection Regulation requires clear and plain language
B. Users are less likely to read it (correct)
C. Users are more likely to grasp the full extent of the data processing
D. Several US laws require clear and conspicuous privacy policies/notices

More information:
Users are more likely to read the privacy notice if they can actually understand it. Therefore, option B is the correct answer since this statement is incorrect.

6. What would be the best moment to show the privacy notice for a consumer software program?
A. During setup
B. Before setup
C. Before purchase (correct)
D. Before first use
More information:
From a privacy perspective, the data subject (consumer) should be informed before the data is processed. From a common sense perspective, this is performed as soon as possible, so before the purchase as this would prevent a consumer from buying something he/she will return later due to not agreeing with the privacy policy (or reluctantly consenting to the privacy policy). Option C is the correct answer. Clarifications on this topic are likely to follow, as there are discussions on the data collection by mobile phone providers, because smartphones can often not be used without accepting the privacy policy.

7. Which of the following is likely not a risk an IT manager has to deal with?
A. Improper access to data
B. Privacy by Design (correct)
C. Data breaches
D. Incorrect retention periods
More information:
Privacy by design is not a risk but a method of incorporating privacy in the design process, hence option D is the correct answer to the question.

Use this case for the following three questions:

Amidst the craze for mobile phone application development, you and a few friends had the brilliant idea to develop an application that allows users to find single people in the area. You develop the application and witness the user base expanding rapidly and the application becoming the most popular dating application worldwide.

You struggle to keep the application online though, as mobile advertisement delivery is cumbersome, and is detrimental to user experience. Due to this, one of the other developers comes with the brilliant idea to analyze the data of users and create a database full of qualities that people in specific areas have.

After setting up meetings with potential buyers for the analysis data, it appears to be a great source of income. The application is stripped of its advertisements for an optimal user experience, and the new update enables the collection of more types of data about the user.

8. Where would the specifics of what is being done be mentioned for the users in the European Union?
A. In the privacy notice, to be made available before starting to collect data (correct)
B. As no consent is required, there is no need to inform the users of the data collection
C. Only the data collection that cannot reasonably be expected needs to be communicated to the user, which may be unnecessary in this case
D. Only for the paid version of the application is such communication required

More information:
The information on the privacy practices needs to be made available at the latest right before processing personal data. Option A is the correct answer, options B, C and D are false.

9. If the application makes decision automatically, such as which users to connect to which other user, what can be said about that practice?
A. This is a form of processing that does not need to be communicated
B. This likely constitutes automated decision-making (correct)
C. If this is a technology-enabled process, it is not processing of personal data since no person is involved
D. A contract with the user is required to continue this practice
More information:
Automated decision-making is referred to in the General Data Protection Regulation and something organizations need to mention in their privacy notice. Option B is the correct answer.

10. When designing the dating application, which of the following would be the best example of Privacy by Design?
A. Allowing a user to stop the application accessing the user's photos
B. Allowing a user to stop the application accessing the user's contacts
C. No unnecessary connections between the application and the user's device (correct)
D. Using a third party for the payment process for the customers that elect to use the paid version of the application

<u>More information:</u>
Privacy by Design should result in processing as little personal data as possible, and result in the lowest risk of a data breach as possible. From the options provided, option C is the correct answer because unnecessary connections likely needlessly increase the chance of a data breach.

11. What is cyphertext best described as?
A. Random data on a hard drive
B. A list of passwords
C. An encryption tool
D. Unreadable seemingly random data (correct)
<u>More information:</u>
Cyphertext is the text that you end up with after encryption. The data seems random, but is the result of using an algorithm and cannot be read as is (you will need the encryption key). Option D is the correct answer.

12. Receiving a text message with a passcode after entering your password is which of the following?
A. Two-way protection
B. Two-way authentication
C. Encrypted transmission
D. Multi-factor authentication (correct)
<u>More information:</u>
Both receiving a text message with a passcode and entering a password (different from the passcode) are ways of authentication. Using more than one way/factor (in this instance two) is called multi-factor authentication.

13. Which of the following best describes encryption?
A. Compressed data
B. Data requiring a key (correct)
C. Randomized data
D. Empty file storage
More information:
A key is required to read the data that has been encrypted, so option B is the correct answer. Option C may seem correct at first read, but encrypted data is not actually random and only seems that way without a key.

14. Which of the following does not refer to access control within an organization?
A. Role-based access control
B. Person-based access control
C. CEO overruling for processing of personal data (correct)
D. Restricting certain levels of the organization from file access
More information:
Options A, B and D clearly pertain to access control as they are about granting access or denying access. Option C is about the processing, which is not necessarily impacting the access to the data. Option C is the correct answer.

15. Which of the following is least likely a risk of the Internet of Things?
A. Persons not being able to request access to their personal data (correct)
B. Accidentally collecting data that is not allowed to be collected
C. Being able to link data to uncover more information inadvertently
D. An inadequate level of risk being assigned to the collected data

More information:
All options presented are risks, but given that if something is personal data, organizations know something about someone and are thus also able to process a data access request. Option A is the correct answer.

16. Which of the following is least likely effective in preventing access to data by an intruder?
A. Poor access controls
B. A virus
C. A password policy (correct)
D. A stolen computer
More information:
A password policy should make passwords difficult to guess or uncover in a different way, such as a brute force attack. This would prevent entry into the network where the files are stored or the computers that contain the files. Option C is the correct answer. If there were poor access controls a guest could likely have access to more than needed, a virus could likely result in automatic sending of files or other alterations and a stolen computer would give the hacker a lot of time to crack the password.

17. What is the most likely risk of over securing data?
A. Attracting hackers to the data
B. Overloading the firewall
C. Ignored access control policies
D. Productivity is reduced (correct)
More information:
If data is over secured, such as an unnecessarily heavy encryption method, the time required to access a file is likely increased unnecessarily. The time to access a file results in delays, which reduces productivity if the files are needed to perform a task. Option D is the correct answer.

18. What is the security advantage of using cables instead of wireless internet?
A. Data transfers can take place at a higher speed
B. An intruder would more likely need physical access in order to intercept data (correct)
C. No firewall is required
D. Password policies can be simplified
More information:
If nothing is sent through the air, nothing can be intercepted through the air. Therefore, a physical action would need to take place to intercept data, which is likely more cumbersome for those looking to intercept and thus a security advantage. Option B is the correct answer.

19. When would an organization most likely use a bastion server?
A. When there are a large number of applications that cannot run only on individual computers (correct)
B. When you wish to enhance security by scanning all incoming data
C. When it is too expensive to install solid-state drives in al computers
D. When access controls need to be applied uniformly for all programs
More information:
A bastion server is a server dedicated to running applications. Option A is the correct answer. It does not necessarily do anything for security, it has nothing to do with solid-state drives and access controls can also be applied uniformly without a bastion server.

20. What is the best way to determine whether a privacy policy applies to a file on the network of an organization?
A. An analysis performed by the Chief Information Security Officer
B. A digital Data Protection Officer signature
C. A server scan on the size and date of the data
D. Classifying the data (correct)
More information:
When classifying data, all kinds of properties are assigned to a file, including whether a certain privacy policy applies and the file can only be processed in a certain way because of it. Option D is the correct answer.

21. How is it most likely called when no names are present in a dataset but linking it with another dataset results in identification of the data subjects in the dataset?
A. Anonymization
B. Pseudonymization (correct)
C. Encryption
D. Compression
More information:
Pseudonymization is still reversible. Hence option B is the correct answer. The General Data Protection Regulation for example, talks about irreversibly anonymized data, for which pseudonymization is not enough.

22. When a video of someone is posted and that person was not the original subject of the video but their face was placed on the original subject, what is this most likely called?
A. A deep fake (correct)
B. A facetime video
C. Corrupted data
D. A data breach

More information:
Deep fake technology swaps the face of one person with that of another in a realistic manner. Option A is the correct answer.

23. Which of the following is an example of a nudge?
A. A login requirement to access your social media account
B. A reminder of the consequences before allowing or starting a process (correct)
C. An IP verification before a social media post gets processed
D. A multi-factor authentication requirement before accessing your social media account
More information:
A nudge is intended for the data subject to be reminded of the consequences of something, for example being aware that everyone in their network can see their post on social media. Option B is the correct answer.

24. Which of the following is not a common privacy dark pattern?
A. Anchoring (correct)
B. Distractions and delays
C. Framing
D. Cumbersome privacy choices
More information:
Anchoring is categorized as a decision heuristic in your study materials, not a privacy dark pattern. Option A is the correct answer.

25. If you are asked, when reacting to an online advertisement, to transfer 1 cent to confirm your identity, but you are sent a fake link so as to lure you into exposing your password, what is that called?
A. Spear phishing
B. Phishing (correct)
C. Spam
D. Malware
More information:
The 1 cent trick is a trick where you are sent a fake link to your bank, tricking you into logging in, which provides the persons behind the sent link with your login information. This is called phishing. Option B is the correct answer. Spear phishing is going for the richer or more high-profile targets, which is not likely the case here, as it involves an advertisement accessible to everyone.

26. Which of the following is most important for anti-malware software?
A. A dedicated server
B. Access to browser history
C. Access to personal data
D. Up-to-date signatures (correct)
More information:
Malware evolves all the time, hence it is important to update your software frequently so that the anti-malware software can detect the newest malware. Option D is the correct answer.

27. In which of the following cases does the IP address of a VPN most likely constitute, or lead to collecting, personal data?
A. When using a VPN to spoof the region so you can access content of a that region
B. When having paid for the access to the VPN with a personal credit card
C. When someone uses a VPN to access their e-mail inbox
D. When only one person uses the VPN (correct)
More information:
If only one person uses the VPN, everything that is registered under that VPN can be linked to one person, likely making it personal data (if the person using it is traceable). Option D is the correct answer. If more people were using the VPN, the logged actions of what happened under the VPN is not necessarily attributable to only one person.

28. What are maximum tries and account lockout?
A. Password heuristics
B. Standard practice
C. Malware protection
D. Authentication rules (correct)
More information:
Maximum tries and account lockout are ways to limit the risk of unauthorized persons accessing an account. They are authentication rules. Option D is the correct answer.

29. What is the most effective way of preventing private data from leaving an organization's server?
A. Using a malware scanner
B. Using a virus scanner
C. Network-level data loss prevention technologies using a scanner (correct)
D. Role-based access control

More information:
Network-level data loss prevention technologies are the most effective of the options provided. It is in the name. Option C is the correct answer, although all of the provided options help in some way.

30. Which of the following describes a zero-day threat?
A. A known weakness in a software package
B. A postponed software update
C. An unsecure http connection as part of a startup protocol
D. An unknown weakness in software (correct)
More information:
Zero-day threats are unknown or unaddressed weaknesses and therefore quite dangerous. Option D is the correct answer. The other options do describe unaddressed/unknown weaknesses. Software updates are very important since they address weaknesses that have been discovered. Although in June 2017 the NotPetya ransomware was spread through a software update, so there are always exceptions.

31. What gets transmitted over a network with VoIP?
A. Voice communication (correct)
B. IP addresses
C. Viruses
D. Virus signatures
More information:
VoIP stands for Voice over IP, which means voice communication is sent over a network. Option A is the correct answer.

32. How can you protect files after they are copied to a different device?
A. Digital Rights Management (correct)
B. Secure transfer
C. Anonymization
D. De-identification
More information:
Digital Rights Management is a technology that can limit the use, modification and distribution of files. Option A is the correct answer. Options C and D would work for personal data.

33. Which of the following is the least likely reason organizations use cloud storage?
A. Enhanced security (correct)
B. Better access to data
C. Lower costs of data storage
D. Improvements in data recovery
More information:
Generally, starting to use cloud storage does not necessarily increase security. This answer implies that the security at the organization is lower than that at the cloud storage provider. Option A is the correct answer. Options B and C are more inherent to cloud storage. Option D is due to the data being on a server rather than only on a disaster-stricken organization's property.

34. Which of the following will privacy policies least likely aid in?
A. Financial risk reduction
B. Security risk reduction (correct)
C. Legal risk reduction
D. Brand risk reduction

More information:
A security policy would be needed to reduce security risks. The others are possible consequences of poor privacy practices and would be served more directly by a privacy policy. Option B is the correct answer.

35. What can be an issue with organizational privacy training?
A. Privacy practices of other teams are not always covered (correct)
B. E-learning is not effective
C. Even after a privacy incident, CEOs are reluctant to approve privacy training
D. If a security training is already in place, there can be a lot of overlap
More information:
Organizations can be large and different departments tend to have their own practices. It is impossible, if privacy is not centrally managed, to cover all these practices during privacy training. Option A is the correct answer.

36. Which of the following does not prevent raw data from being accessed?
A. Homomorphic encryption
B. Multiparty computation
C. Differential privacy
D. Compression (correct)
More information:
Compression does not necessarily prevent the raw data from being accessed. Passwords can be used, but then it is more than just compression. Option D is the correct answer.

37. Which of the following permits defining group policies?
A. HTTPS
B. HTTP
C. Microsoft SQL (correct)
D. Virtual Private Network
More information:
Microsoft SQL is a relational database management system and allows for defining group policies. Option C is the correct answer.

38. What is COBIT5?
A. A standard for privacy policies
B. A standard for privacy notices
C. A guide for 256-bit encryption
D. A framework of security controls (correct)
More information:
Control Objectives for Information and Related Technologies (COBIT) is a framework of security controls created by the Information Systems Audit and Control Association. Option D is the correct answer.

39. Which of the following will you least likely find in an organization's privacy notice?
A. The type of data collected
B. How to make use of your rights
C. Where a complaint can be made
D. The privacy officer of the processor (correct)
More information:
According to the General Data Protection Regulation, (types of) third parties (which includes processors) should be made known to the data subject. The privacy officer of a third party is not required to be communicated, and is not likely to be present in a privacy notice. Option D is the correct answer.

40. When a website allows you to click on the topics you want information on, what is this likely called?
A. A privacy policy
B. A layered privacy notice (correct)
C. A cookie wall
D. Privacy Icons
More information:
A layered privacy notice does not deliver all the information at once, but only the information relevant or requested. This is an example of layered privacy notice, so option B is the correct answer.

41. What can a privacy policy do for an organization that develops one?
A. Identify privacy gaps within an organization
B. Ensure compliance with relevant legislation
C. Set the tone across the organization (correct)
D. Prevent data breaches and fines
More information:
A privacy policy (not the notice) generally sets the tone by defining responsibilities and privacy goals. Option C is the correct answer. The other options are (hopefully) the indirect result.

42. What is an agreement with a third-party processing data on an organization's behalf called?
A. Binding Corporate Rules
B. A binding privacy agreement
C. A data processing agreement (correct)
D. A contractor agreement
More information:
This type of contract, as required by the General Data Protection Regulation, is generally referred to as a data processing agreement. Option C is the correct answer.

43. Under the General Data Protection Regulation, how many days does an organization have, to respond to a data access request?
A. Twenty-five days
B. Twenty working days
C. A month (correct)
D. Two months
More information:
An organization has a month to respond to a data request. Extensions are possible, but there needs to be a good reason. Option C is the correct answer.

44. What can the act of labelling a file high, moderate of low be considered?
A. Data classification (correct)
B. Processing of personal data
C. Processing of personal information
D. Data collection
More information:
Assigning a level of risk, required level of protection, etcetera is considered data classification. Option A is the correct answer.

Use this case for the following three question:

A new video streaming service is providing customers with free trials for a limited time. They do this in the testing phase, and also specify to the customers that the streaming service is still in the testing phase.

During the testing phase, a large amount of new content is delivered to the first users in the form of TV shows and movies. The streaming service uses all kinds of data from the users to analyze the performance of its service, as well as the quality of its content.

One of the ways the streaming service uses users for determining the quality of its content, is by accessing the camera in the smart TV, laptop or mobile device of the user. The application of the streaming service contains emotion-recognition software, which analyses the facial expressions of the users. This is then sent as feedback, as a replacement of organizing a focus group.

45. What kind of data is the facial recognition software processing?
A. Biometric data (correct)
B. Physical data
C. Legal data
D. Digital imagery
More information:
Facial recognition software uses unique features of someone's face, which can be considered biometric data. Option A is the correct answer.

46. A group of hackers accessed the servers of the streaming service and has stolen a large amount of user data. Which of the following is likely true?
A. Since the streaming service was free, no guarantees can be provided for the user's privacy, and there are no legal obligations resting on the streaming service
B. If the hackers are paid to delete the data, no further action is required
C. The streaming service has to organize a press conference to inform the public
D. The streaming service will have to report this to a Data Protection Authority (correct)
More information:
Data breaches have to be reported, under certain circumstances. Given the large number of members that the streaming service likely has, as well as the global scale on which they operate, there is likely legislation requiring to report this data breach. An example is the General Data Protection Regulation in the European Union, which would likely require this to be reported due to the large number of data subjects it pertains to and the biometric data that is possibly linked to each user. Option D is the correct answer.

47. For the storage of the results of the analysis as regards viewing history, which of the following is likely required in the European Union?
A. Consent is required (correct)
B. A data processing agreement is required
C. No processors may be used
D. Storage is not processing, so only storing the data without further use requires no action

More information:
Consent may be required, but not necessarily as many factors are unknown. However, the other options are not true, which leads to option A as the correct answer.

48. When only certain types of employees have access to certain data, what is this called?
A. Multi-factor authentication
B. Role-based access control (correct)
C. Three prong authentication
D. Person-based access control
More information:
A type of employee can be said to be a role, and therefore the question was aiming at role-based access control. Option B is the correct answer.

49. What is the period of an organization's data retention least likely influenced by?
A. Processing requirements
B. Organization resources (correct)
C. Regulatory requirements
D. Data classification
More information:
Retention includes both storage and deletion. Since it has already been stored, an organization's resources are not likely a hindrance. For deletion, an organization's resources are not allowed to form a hindrance if there is a legal retention period. Option B is the correct answer, as a retention period or retention capacity should not rely on an organization's resources.

50. How can data aggregation best be described?
A. The scrambling of data to make it unreadable without a key
B. The removal of names
C. The removal of all identifiers in a dataset
D. A reflection of attributes with a certain level of granularity (correct)
More information:
Data aggregation is the grouping of specific elements of a dataset and thereby likely (but not necessarily) removing identifying factors, resulting in a reflection of attributes with a certain level of granularity. Option D is the correct answer.

51. Which of the following is least likely a risk when deleting data in an organization?
A. That an update in the data inventory is required due to the deleted data (correct)
B. That the data is present at other points in the organization
C. That there is still a legal requirement to keep the data
D. That a copy exists in a backup
More information:
When deleting data, this does not mean an update in the processing inventory is required. The deletion should bee foreseen, as the data inventory likely contains a retention period for the personal data with which the processing takes place. Option A is the correct answer, the others are valid risks.

52. Which of the following is the least likely risk if an organization loses data stored on a thumb drive?
A. A data breach for data with lower levels of encryption
B. Permanent loss of data due to not having a backup (correct)
C. Being left with outdated data
D. Losing track and not obliging with a request for deletion

More information:
A thumb drive itself is usually a backup, slightly updated version or copy of something. Working only on a thumb drive is quite rare (and not recommended). Therefore, even if the thumb drive is lost, there is likely still a (recent) copy of the data somewhere. Option B is the correct answer.

53. How can a browser be identified based on its unique settings?
A. VPN spoofing
B. Browser fingerprinting (correct)
C. A malware infection
D. Through an Internet Explored Exploit
More information:
Browser fingerprinting uses the unique settings of a browser to identify the visitor of a website. This includes accidental changes, such as scrolling while pressing control, so be careful. Option B is the correct answer.

54. When only users from a certain location can access a file, what is this called?
A. Geo-favoring
B. Virtual Private Network
C. Two-factor authentication
D. Attribute-based access control (correct)
More information:
Location is an attribute, hence this is attribute-based access control. Only the location is used for the control in this situation, thus it is not multi-factor authentication. Option D is the correct answer.

55. What are Secure Sockets Layer and Transport Layer Security?
A. These are website tools
B. These are persistent cookies
C. These are functional cookies
D. These are types of protocols (correct)
More information:
SSL and TLS are cryptographic protocols that ensure only the sender and receiver of the information can read it. Option D is the correct answer.

56. Which of the following results in data that cannot be decrypted?
A. Asymmetric encryption
B. Symmetric encryption
C. Hashing (correct)
D. Compression
More information:
Hashing is a way to change data so that it cannot be decrypted. This is often used for passwords, which is something that you will need to remember for the exam (in addition to what salting is). Option C is the correct answer.

57. When you are at work and login once, providing you with access to e-mail, work-time registration, etcetera, what is this generally referred to?
A. Multi-factor authentication
B. Multi-platform authentication
C. Single-sign on (correct)
D. Multi-user authentication
More information:
Single-sign on allows you to login once, which then gives you access to other environments where you would normally also be required to login. Option C is the correct answer.

58. What is a brute force attack, with current (2020) level technology, most useful for?
A. Cracking simple passwords (correct)
B. Matching asymmetric encryption keys
C. Deciphering encryption
D. Generating cheat codes for new gaming consoles
More information:
A brute force attack can be explained in a simplified way as letting a computer keep trying to guess. For passwords this is often used. The simpler the password, the more easily it is guessed through a brute force attack. Option A is the correct answer.

59. Which of the following statements is least true about incident response in a typical organization?
A. The Data Protection Officer runs the show after an incident (correct)
B. It is a joint effort to guide the organization in the correct response
C. Privacy is not necessarily the most important part of the incident response strategy
D. It is the head of the organization that ultimately decides which course to take
More information:
Data Protection is important, but the Data Protection Officer's role does not necessarily include running the show during an incident. The Data Protection Officer will most likely assume a more advisory role. Option A is the correct answer.

60. Which of the following is most important for the systems development lifecycle from a General Data Protection Regulation perspective?
A. Approval of the Data Protection Officer
B. Involvement of the Data Protection Officer
C. Privacy by Design (correct)
D. A Privacy Impact Assessment
More information:
Of the options provided, Privacy by Design is required by the General Data Protection Regulation. Option C is the correct answer. The others are not required, and a Privacy Impact Assessment is not mentioned in the General Data Protection Regulation (Data Protection Impact Assessments are though).

61. Which of the following is not a way for an organization to address privacy risk?
A. Transfer
B. Assess (correct)
C. Accept
D. Mitigate
More information:
Assessing does not address the risk, it merely assesses it. The other options are actions directed at the risk. Option B is the correct answer.

62. Which of the following is true about the Personal Information Protection and Electronic Documents Act?
A. Organizations must obtain at least opt-out consent before processing (correct)
B. The Personal Information Protection and Electronic Documents Act applies only to government agencies
C. The Personal Information Protection and Electronic Documents Act is a South African law
D. The Personal Information Protection and Electronic Documents Act is a Singaporean law
More information:
The Personal Information Protection and Electronic Documents Act is a Canadian law, applying to the private sector. It requires organizations to obtain (at least) opt-out consent before processing (unless an exception applies). Option A is the correct answer.

63. Which of the following is not part of the information lifecycle?
A. Retention
B. Destruction
C. Consent (correct)
D. Use
More information:
Use, Retention and Destruction are part of the information lifecycle. Consent is not part of the information lifecycle, so option C is the correct answer.

64. IT security measures in an organization likely have the most impact on which of the following?
A. Use limitation
B. Data quality
C. Accountability
D. Security safeguards (correct)

More information:
IT security measures are security safeguards. Therefore option D is the correct answer, as that is where the most impact is in this case.

65. Which of the following types of cookies most likely does not require consent?
A. Functional cookies (correct)
B. Analytical cookies
C. Marketing cookies
D. Tracking cookies
More information:
Functional cookies are essential to making a website function as it should. The other cookies are not necessary for the functioning of the website (unless embedded links require them of course). Option A is the correct answer.

66. What is the most likely reason for choosing a reputable third party to procure data from?
A. Data security
B. Collection limitation
C. The correct legal basis
D. Data quality (correct)
More information:
Data quality is important. Therefore, option D is the correct answer. Option A is not required at this step in the process, as you are choosing. Option B is not relevant, as this would be the third party's concern (assuming the data has already been collected and is allowed to be sold). Option C should have been figured out before deciding to process, or is irrelevant if the data does not contain personal data.

67. When requesting a third party, in the European Union, to collect information about local individuals for your organization which of the following is not necessarily important?
A. A Data Protection Officer (correct)
B. Adequate security
C. A privacy Notice
D. A data processing agreement
More information:
Data Protection Officers are only mandatory in certain instances. Therefore, option A is the correct answer as it is not necessarily important.

68. Which of the following is true for personal data that has fulfilled the purpose it was collected for?
A. It can be kept only if consent is provided
B. System limitations provide a valid reason to postpone deletion
C. It can be stored up to 10 years
D. There is likely no legal basis for further processing in its current form (correct)
More information:
When the collection purpose has been fulfilled there is likely no legal basis for further processing (unless one shows up, such as scientific research). It would of course not be fair to collect data informing the data subject about what it is used for, and then also using it for something else. Option D is the correct answer.

69. Which of the following is least likely deduced from a person's web browsing history?
A. Employment status
B. Sexual preference
C. Medical condition
D. Exact financial data (correct)

More information:
From which websites are visited you can figure out if someone is likely rich or poor, but not exactly how much money a person has. It can be seen that someone has visited his/her bank's website, but not the content of the bank account. Option D is the correct answer. The other options can be figured out from the types of website someone visits.

70. Which of the following can be said about hard copies containing personal data?
A. They are unregulated as they are not digital
B. No security is possible as there cannot be an audit trail
C. They can be part of a data breach (correct)
D. They fall outside the scope of the General Data Protection Regulation
More information:
Hard copies can still be in scope of the General Data Protection Regulation and can therefore be part of a data breach. Option C is the correct answer.

71. What is likely the best way to test software that processes personal data?
A. Use data without names
B. Acquire consent for testing
C. Encrypt the data before testing
D. Use dummy data (correct)
More information:
All functions of the software need to be tested so as to make sure it processes personal data properly. Therefore, a set of dummy data needs to be created. Consent would not address any risks, taking away names might not allow for full functionality testing and encrypting the data would result in data unreadable for the software. Option D is the correct answer.

72. When composing a transfer agreement, from a privacy perspective, which of the following is the most important element?
A. The processing fee
B. The file types used
C. The processing limitations (correct)
D. The encryption method
More information:
When the data is transferred to a third party, it must be assured that any personal data is only processed respecting the data subjects' rights, meaning limiting the processing to ways that do not break any laws. Option C is the correct answer.

73. Which of the following best describes a data retention period?
A. The maximum period of time data should be kept (correct)
B. A set time to destruct the data
C. A set time before encryption
D. Storage space
More information:
A retention period is the time the data should be kept, or is allowed to be processed. Option A is the correct answer. Option B may be partially correct, but takes the focus away from the retention itself.

74. Which of the following is most true about business continuity and disaster recovery strategies?
A. They require Data Protection Officer approval
B. Most privacy laws require at least one of the two
C. They must be continually reviewed (correct)
D. Most privacy laws require both

More information:
There are many changes an organization faces, such as new technological developments, new legal developments and new organizational developments. This brings with it new threats and new expectations. Therefore, continuous review is important. Option C is the correct answer.

75. Which of the following is least likely going to cause a new issue when starting to use data centers instead of one local server?
A. The encryption method used to protect the data (correct)
B. The legislation that has become applicable
C. Physical security of the data centers
D. Data processing agreements, if outsourced
More information:
The encryption on a local server is likely the same as the encryption an organization would use for the same data in a data center. Option A is the correct answer.

76. When can data about the functioning of a vendor be considered personal data under the General Data Protection Regulation?
A. When there is only one employee working for that company (correct)
B. When no data processing agreement is in place
C. When a lower standard of encryption is used
D. The moment consent is obtained
More information:
When a company consists of only one employee, whatever relates to that company relates almost directly to that one employee. Option A is the correct answer.

Use this case for the following three question:

A virus breaks out in Asia. The virus is dangerous to the elderly but spreads through people of all ages. Slowly, the virus is spreading from Asia to the rest of the world and starts claiming lives.

As a result of the virus people are frantic and overly cautious. This has led to people calling in sick, not going to school or work. Public spaces are becoming deserted as well, and the economy is slowly crumbling, small business owners being the first to collapse.

To combat the loss in productivity, many of the larger organizations are asking their employees to work from home. They provide teleworking equipment, either to be installed on their own personal computer or on a computer the organization provides.

77. In order to establish a secure connection, a program is provided that connects to the organization's network and through that connects to the internet, making it appear as if the IP address used by the employees is the IP address of the organization. What can this be called?
A. Multi-factor authentication
B. Network spoofing
C. IP address masking
D. The use of a VPN (correct)
More information:
The situation described is a VPN connection. Option D is the correct answer.

78. An external server hosts all working documents that employees need to do their job, which all can access at the same time from a distance. What can the storage on an external server be called?
A. Encryption
B. Intranet
C. File access audit trail
D. Cloud computing (correct)
More information:
Storage on an external server is a form of cloud computing. Option D is the correct answer.

79. When using a company provided computer, the webcam in the laptop is accessible to the company's IT personnel. Where would this information most likely be found?
A. In the employment contract
B. In a privacy notice provided with the company computer (correct)
C. In labor law
D. In the organization's privacy policy
More information:
If the company is able to monitor its employees through the webcam of their computer, this is something that is likely mentioned in the privacy notice provided with the computer. The other options would likely not directly contain information this specific. Option B is the correct answer.

80. Which is not a commonly used form of authentication?
A. Something you know
B. Something you have
C. Where you are
D. Metadata (correct)

More information:
Metadata is data about data, and not something commonly used as authentication. Option D is the correct answer.

81. Which of the following is not a single sign-on technology?
A. OpenID Federation
B. Liberty Alliance
C. Identity Metasystem Architecture
D. Microsoft Access (correct)
More information:
Microsoft Access is part of Microsoft Office and has nothing to do with single sign-on. Option D is the correct answer. The way to correctly answer this question here is not that you know what Microsoft Access is, but that you know the names of single sign-on technology mentioned in your study materials.

82. Which of the following is an example of Software as a Service?
A. Windows 10
B. Software on a USB drive
C. Office 365 (correct)
D. Software downloaded from the cloud to install
More information:
Microsoft Office 365 is an example of an application that runs in the cloud. Option D may trick some people, but when it is only downloaded and then installed it is not Software as a Service. Option C is the correct answer.

83. What is an example of a demilitarized zone network?
A. Public WIFI
B. A third amendment server
C. A pay network
D. A store's separate network for customers only (correct)

More information:
A demilitarized zone network adds an additional layer of security to the store's network. This is established by not connecting the customers to the store's primary network, but to a separate network. Option D is the correct answer.

84. Which of the following is a pass phrase?
A. @lRightyTh3n
B. 124590MAX
C. Milkwaukee
D. HappyDayCongruencyHorse (correct)
More information:
A pass phrase is a phrase used as a password. The idea is that it will be long and in an order that does not make sense but is easy to remember. Option D is the correct answer.

85. A fingerprint is an example of which of the following?
A. Biometrics (correct)
B. Multi-factor authentication
C. Password replacement
D. Location data
More information:
Fingerprints are an example of biometric data. Option A is the correct answer.

86. Which of the following is an example of the privacy paradox?
A. Staying away from all social media because you do not want your data shared
B. Opting out of location tracking on social media, but publicly checking-in to every hotel and restaurant you visit (correct)
C. Not allowing a social media application to access your photos, but having over a terabyte of photos on your mobile device
D. Refusing to share your sexual preference on a social media website, but then joining another social media website specific for a certain sexual preference
More information:
Option B describes an example of the privacy paradox as publicly checking-in to hotels and restaurants also captures the locations you have visited. Option D may seem correct, but here the websites are likely operated by different owners and do not communicate with each other.

87. What gets inserted during an SQL injection?
A. Commands (correct)
B. A form
C. Malware
D. Executable files
More information:
An SQL injection injects commands. Option A is the correct answer. Only superficial knowledge of SQL injections is required for the exam.

88. What can most likely be said about web beacons?
A. Web beacons cannot track you
B. Web beacons are exactly the same as a cookie
C. A web beacon is malware
D. Web beacons are not visible to the naked eye (correct)

More information:
Web beacons are usually not visible to the naked eye. They are transparent pixels that load and send your IP address to a third party. Option D is the correct answer.

89. If your web browser allows for the option to send a signal not to place tracking cookies, what would this be called?
A. Privacy by Design
B. Opt-in
C. Opt-out
D. Do Not Track (correct)
More information:
This is a Do Not Track request. It is not necessarily privacy by design, but would be if the signal would be sent unless turned off. Option D is the correct answer.

90. How can cloud computing best be described?
A. Third party involved processing
B. Local Area Network
C. Using servers on the internet to do your work (correct)
D. Storage expansion
More information:
Cloud computing entails using external servers. Option C is the correct answer. There are not necessarily third parties involved, and it does not necessarily involve storage.

Made in the USA
Monee, IL
27 August 2020